50 The Ultimate Italian Cookbook Recipes

By: Kelly Johnson

Table of Contents

- Margherita Pizza
- Authentic Spaghetti Carbonara
- Creamy Risotto alla Milanese
- Homemade Fettuccine Alfredo
- Sicilian Eggplant Caponata
- Traditional Osso Buco
- Tuscan Ribollita Soup
- Classic Lasagna Bolognese
- Homemade Ricotta Gnocchi
- Veal Saltimbocca
- Traditional Panzanella Salad
- Lemon Chicken Piccata
- Seafood Cioppino
- Beef Braciole in Tomato Sauce
- Fresh Caprese Salad
- Spinach and Ricotta Stuffed Ravioli
- Creamy Burrata with Fresh Tomatoes
- Slow-Cooked Beef Ragu
- Traditional Tiramisu
- Florentine Steak (Bistecca alla Fiorentina)
- Wild Mushroom Risotto
- Pistachio Panna Cotta
- Penne alla Vodka
- Zucchini Parmigiana
- Eggplant Involtini
- Fennel and Orange Salad
- Garlic and Herb Focaccia Bread
- Polenta with Sausage and Mushrooms
- Shrimp Scampi Linguine
- Arancini di Riso (Rice Balls)
- Chicken Cacciatore
- Prosciutto-Wrapped Melon
- Amaretto Biscotti
- Lemon Ricotta Cheesecake
- Basil Pesto Genovese

- Creamy Potato Gnocchi with Gorgonzola Sauce
- Calabrian Chili Oil Pasta
- Grilled Octopus Salad
- Clam and Mussel Linguine
- Sweet Ricotta Cannoli
- Pumpkin Ravioli with Sage Butter
- Porcini Mushroom Tagliatelle
- Classic Minestrone Soup
- Marinated Artichokes
- Italian Wedding Soup
- Stuffed Bell Peppers with Italian Sausage
- Ricotta-Stuffed Zucchini Blossoms
- Chocolate-Hazelnut Gelato
- Chicken Marsala
- Amatriciana Pasta

Margherita Pizza

Ingredients:

- 1 ball of pizza dough
- 1/2 cup tomato sauce (preferably San Marzano)
- 8 oz fresh mozzarella, sliced
- Fresh basil leaves
- 1-2 tbsp olive oil
- Salt to taste

Instructions:

1. Preheat your oven to the highest setting (450-500°F) and place a pizza stone or baking sheet inside to heat.
2. Roll out the pizza dough into a 10-12 inch circle.
3. Spread the tomato sauce evenly over the dough, leaving a small border around the edges.
4. Distribute mozzarella slices over the sauce.
5. Slide the pizza onto the preheated stone or baking sheet and bake for 7-10 minutes, until the crust is golden and the cheese is bubbly.
6. Remove from the oven, garnish with fresh basil leaves, and drizzle with olive oil.
7. Slice and serve hot.

Spaghetti Carbonara

Ingredients:

- 400g (14 oz) spaghetti
- 150g (5 oz) guanciale, diced (or pancetta as an alternative)
- 4 large eggs
- 100g (3.5 oz) Pecorino Romano cheese, finely grated
- Freshly cracked black pepper
- Salt for pasta water

Instructions:

1. **Cook the Spaghetti**:
   - Bring a large pot of salted water to a boil. Cook the spaghetti according to package directions until al dente. Reserve 1 cup of pasta cooking water before draining the pasta.
2. **Prepare the Guanciale**:
   - While the pasta cooks, heat a large skillet over medium heat. Add the diced guanciale and cook until it becomes crispy and releases its fat, about 4–5 minutes. Remove from the heat and set aside.
3. **Make the Carbonara Sauce**:
   - In a mixing bowl, beat the eggs and combine with the grated Pecorino Romano cheese. Add a generous amount of freshly cracked black pepper. The mixture should be creamy and smooth.
4. **Combine the Pasta and Sauce**:
   - Once the pasta is cooked and drained, quickly add it to the skillet with the guanciale (off the heat to avoid scrambling the eggs). Pour the egg and cheese mixture over the pasta and toss vigorously to coat the pasta in the sauce. If the sauce seems too thick, add a little reserved pasta water until you reach a silky, creamy consistency.
5. **Serve**:
   - Divide the carbonara among plates. Top with additional Pecorino Romano and black pepper to taste. Serve immediately while hot.

Creamy Risotto alla Milanese

Ingredients:

- 1 ½ cups Arborio rice
- 4 cups chicken broth
- 2 tbsp unsalted butter
- 1 small onion, finely chopped
- 1/2 cup dry white wine
- ½ tsp saffron threads
- ¾ cup grated Parmesan cheese
- Salt and pepper to taste

Instructions:

1. Warm the chicken broth in a saucepan. Add saffron threads and let them infuse.
2. In a large pan, melt butter and sauté onions until translucent.
3. Add the rice and stir to coat with butter. Pour in the white wine and cook until evaporated.
4. Gradually add the hot broth, one ladle at a time, stirring frequently until absorbed before adding more broth.
5. Continue until the rice is tender and creamy, about 18–20 minutes.
6. Stir in Parmesan cheese and season with salt and pepper.
7. Serve hot, garnished with extra cheese if desired.

Homemade Fettuccine Alfredo

Ingredients:

- 400g fettuccine pasta
- 1 cup heavy cream
- ½ cup unsalted butter
- 1 cup freshly grated Parmesan cheese
- Salt and pepper to taste
- Fresh parsley, chopped (optional)

Instructions:

1. Cook fettuccine according to package instructions. Drain, reserving some pasta water.
2. In a large pan, melt butter over medium heat and add heavy cream. Bring to a simmer.
3. Add Parmesan cheese and stir until the sauce thickens.
4. Toss the cooked fettuccine in the sauce, adding a little pasta water if needed to loosen.
5. Season with salt and pepper, and serve with fresh parsley.

Sicilian Eggplant Caponata

Ingredients:

- 2 medium eggplants, cubed
- 1 onion, chopped
- 2 celery stalks, chopped
- 1 red bell pepper, chopped
- 1 can (14.5 oz) diced tomatoes
- 2 tbsp red wine vinegar
- 1 tbsp sugar
- 1/4 cup green olives, pitted and chopped
- 2 tbsp capers, drained
- Salt and pepper to taste
- Olive oil for frying

Instructions:

1. Fry the eggplant cubes in olive oil until golden and tender. Set aside.
2. In the same pan, sauté onion, celery, and red bell pepper until softened.
3. Add tomatoes, vinegar, sugar, olives, and capers. Stir to combine.
4. Add fried eggplant back into the pan and cook for 10 minutes, allowing flavors to meld.
5. Season with salt and pepper. Serve warm or at room temperature.

Traditional Osso Buco

Ingredients:

- 4 veal shanks
- 2 tbsp olive oil
- 1 onion, chopped
- 1 carrot, chopped
- 1 celery stalk, chopped
- 2 cloves garlic, minced
- 1 cup white wine
- 2 cups chicken broth
- 1 can (14.5 oz) diced tomatoes
- 1 tsp dried thyme
- 2 bay leaves
- Salt and pepper to taste

Instructions:

1. Heat olive oil in a large pot and brown the veal shanks on all sides. Remove and set aside.
2. In the same pot, sauté onion, carrot, celery, and garlic until softened.
3. Add wine, deglaze the pot, and cook until the wine reduces by half.
4. Add broth, tomatoes, thyme, and bay leaves. Return veal to the pot.
5. Cover and simmer for 1.5–2 hours until the veal is tender.
6. Season with salt and pepper, and serve hot with gremolata.

Tuscan Ribollita Soup

Ingredients:

- 1 tbsp olive oil
- 1 onion, chopped
- 2 carrots, chopped
- 2 celery stalks, chopped
- 2 cloves garlic, minced
- 2 cups cannellini beans, cooked
- 6 cups vegetable broth
- 1 bunch kale, chopped
- 1 can (14.5 oz) diced tomatoes
- 4 cups day-old bread, cubed
- Salt and pepper to taste

Instructions:

1. In a large pot, heat olive oil and sauté onion, carrots, celery, and garlic until softened.
2. Add beans, broth, tomatoes, and kale. Bring to a boil, then simmer for 30 minutes.
3. Add bread cubes and cook for another 15 minutes until the bread breaks down and thickens the soup.
4. Season with salt and pepper. Serve with a drizzle of olive oil.

Classic Lasagna Bolognese

Ingredients:

- 12 lasagna noodles
- 2 cups Bolognese sauce
- 1 ½ cups ricotta cheese
- 1 egg
- 2 cups mozzarella cheese, shredded
- 1 cup Parmesan cheese, grated
- Salt and pepper to taste

Instructions:

1. Preheat oven to 375°F (190°C).
2. Cook the lasagna noodles according to package instructions. Drain and set aside.
3. In a bowl, mix ricotta cheese with egg, salt, and pepper.
4. In a baking dish, layer noodles, Bolognese sauce, ricotta mixture, mozzarella, and Parmesan. Repeat layers.
5. Top with remaining mozzarella and Parmesan, and bake for 45 minutes until bubbly and golden.

Homemade Ricotta Gnocchi

Ingredients:

- 1 ½ cups ricotta cheese
- 1 cup all-purpose flour
- 1 egg
- Salt to taste
- ½ cup Parmesan cheese, grated

Instructions:

1. Combine ricotta, flour, egg, salt, and Parmesan in a bowl. Mix until a dough forms.
2. Roll the dough into small logs and cut into bite-sized pieces.
3. Boil gnocchi in salted water until they float to the surface, about 2–3 minutes.
4. Serve with your favorite sauce, such as a simple butter and sage sauce.

Veal Saltimbocca

Ingredients:

- 4 veal cutlets
- 8 sage leaves
- 4 slices prosciutto
- 1 tbsp olive oil
- ½ cup white wine
- 1 tbsp butter
- Salt and pepper to taste

Instructions:

1. Place a sage leaf on each veal cutlet and top with prosciutto. Secure with toothpicks.
2. Heat olive oil in a pan and cook the veal for 3-4 minutes per side, until golden.
3. Remove veal and deglaze the pan with wine, scraping up any brown bits.
4. Add butter and stir until the sauce thickens.
5. Return veal to the pan, simmer for 2-3 minutes, and season with salt and pepper. Serve hot.

Traditional Panzanella Salad

Ingredients:

- 4 cups day-old bread, cubed
- 2 cups cherry tomatoes, halved
- 1 cucumber, sliced
- 1 red onion, thinly sliced
- ½ cup fresh basil, chopped
- ¼ cup red wine vinegar
- ½ cup extra virgin olive oil
- Salt and pepper to taste

Instructions:

1. Toast the cubed bread in the oven at 375°F (190°C) for 10 minutes, until crispy but still slightly chewy.
2. In a large bowl, combine the toasted bread, tomatoes, cucumber, onion, and basil.
3. In a small bowl, whisk together the red wine vinegar, olive oil, salt, and pepper.
4. Pour the dressing over the salad and toss gently. Let the salad sit for 10 minutes to allow the flavors to meld before serving.

Lemon Chicken Piccata

Ingredients:

- 4 boneless, skinless chicken breasts
- ½ cup flour
- Salt and pepper to taste
- 4 tbsp butter
- 4 tbsp olive oil
- 1 cup chicken broth
- 1 lemon, thinly sliced
- 2 tbsp capers
- Fresh parsley, chopped (for garnish)

Instructions:

1. Pound the chicken breasts to an even thickness. Season with salt and pepper, then dredge in flour.
2. In a large skillet, heat 2 tbsp of butter and 2 tbsp of olive oil over medium-high heat.
3. Cook the chicken for 4–5 minutes per side until golden and cooked through. Remove and set aside.
4. In the same skillet, add chicken broth, lemon slices, and capers. Bring to a simmer.
5. Stir in the remaining butter, then return the chicken to the skillet to coat with the sauce.
6. Garnish with fresh parsley and serve immediately.

Seafood Cioppino

Ingredients:

- 1 lb shrimp, peeled and deveined
- 1 lb clams, scrubbed
- 1 lb mussels, scrubbed
- 1 lb firm white fish (such as cod), cut into chunks
- 1 onion, chopped
- 1 bell pepper, chopped
- 2 cloves garlic, minced
- 1 can (14.5 oz) crushed tomatoes
- 1 ½ cups white wine
- 2 cups fish stock
- 2 tbsp olive oil
- 1 tsp dried oregano
- 1 tsp red pepper flakes
- Salt and pepper to taste
- Fresh parsley, chopped (for garnish)

Instructions:

1. Heat olive oil in a large pot. Add onion, bell pepper, and garlic, sautéing until softened.
2. Stir in crushed tomatoes, wine, fish stock, oregano, and red pepper flakes. Bring to a boil, then reduce heat and simmer for 20 minutes.
3. Add the shrimp, clams, mussels, and fish to the pot. Cover and cook for 5-7 minutes, or until the seafood is cooked through and the clams and mussels have opened.
4. Season with salt and pepper to taste, garnish with fresh parsley, and serve with crusty bread.

Beef Braciole in Tomato Sauce

Ingredients:

- 4 beef steaks (flank or sirloin), pounded thin
- ½ cup breadcrumbs
- ½ cup grated Parmesan cheese
- 2 tbsp fresh parsley, chopped
- 2 cloves garlic, minced
- Salt and pepper to taste
- 1 egg, beaten
- 2 tbsp olive oil
- 2 cups marinara sauce
- 1 tbsp dried oregano
- 1 tbsp fresh basil, chopped

Instructions:

1. Preheat oven to 350°F (175°C). Season the beef steaks with salt and pepper.
2. In a small bowl, mix breadcrumbs, Parmesan, parsley, garlic, and egg. Spoon the mixture onto each beef steak and roll them up tightly. Secure with toothpicks.
3. In a large skillet, heat olive oil over medium-high heat. Brown the beef rolls on all sides, then remove and set aside.
4. In the same skillet, pour in marinara sauce, oregano, and basil. Bring to a simmer.
5. Add the beef rolls back into the sauce, cover, and simmer for 1–1.5 hours, until tender. Serve hot with extra sauce.

Fresh Caprese Salad

Ingredients:

- 4 ripe tomatoes, sliced
- 8 oz fresh mozzarella cheese, sliced
- ¼ cup fresh basil leaves
- ¼ cup extra virgin olive oil
- 2 tbsp balsamic glaze
- Salt and pepper to taste

Instructions:

1. Arrange the tomato and mozzarella slices alternately on a platter.
2. Tuck fresh basil leaves between the slices.
3. Drizzle with olive oil and balsamic glaze.
4. Season with salt and pepper, and serve immediately.

Spinach and Ricotta Stuffed Ravioli

Ingredients for the Filling:

- 2 cups fresh spinach, cooked and squeezed dry
- 1 cup ricotta cheese
- 1 egg
- ½ cup Parmesan cheese, grated
- Salt and pepper to taste

Ingredients for the Pasta Dough:

- 2 cups all-purpose flour
- 2 eggs
- 1 tbsp olive oil
- A pinch of salt

Instructions:

1. For the filling, chop the cooked spinach and mix with ricotta, egg, Parmesan, salt, and pepper.
2. For the dough, combine flour, eggs, olive oil, and salt in a food processor. Pulse until a dough forms, then knead until smooth. Let rest for 30 minutes.
3. Roll out the dough on a floured surface and cut into squares. Place a spoonful of filling in the center of each square.
4. Fold the dough over the filling and press to seal. Boil the ravioli in salted water for 2–3 minutes, until they float.
5. Serve with marinara sauce or brown butter.

Creamy Burrata with Fresh Tomatoes

Ingredients:

- 2 burrata balls
- 4 ripe tomatoes, sliced
- 1 tbsp olive oil
- Fresh basil leaves
- Salt and pepper to taste

Instructions:

1. Arrange the burrata balls on a platter, surrounding them with tomato slices.
2. Drizzle with olive oil and season with salt and pepper.
3. Garnish with fresh basil leaves and serve immediately.

Slow-Cooked Beef Ragu

Ingredients:

- 2 lbs beef chuck roast
- 1 onion, chopped
- 2 carrots, chopped
- 2 celery stalks, chopped
- 4 cloves garlic, minced
- 1 can (14.5 oz) diced tomatoes
- 2 cups beef broth
- 1 tbsp dried oregano
- 2 bay leaves
- Salt and pepper to taste
- Olive oil for searing

Instructions:

1. Heat olive oil in a large pan and brown the beef chuck roast on all sides. Remove and set aside.
2. In the same pan, sauté onion, carrot, celery, and garlic until softened.
3. Transfer the vegetables and beef to a slow cooker. Add diced tomatoes, beef broth, oregano, and bay leaves.
4. Cover and cook on low for 6–8 hours, until the beef is tender and shreds easily.
5. Shred the beef and stir into the sauce. Season with salt and pepper, and serve over pasta or polenta.

Traditional Tiramisu

Ingredients:

- 1 ½ cups strong brewed coffee, cooled
- 3 tbsp dark rum or Marsala wine (optional)
- 6 large egg yolks
- ¾ cup granulated sugar
- 1 ¼ cups mascarpone cheese
- 1 ½ cups heavy cream
- 1 pack ladyfingers
- Cocoa powder for dusting
- Dark chocolate shavings (optional)

Instructions:

1. In a shallow dish, combine brewed coffee and rum (if using). Dip the ladyfingers quickly in the coffee mixture and arrange them in a 9x13 inch dish.
2. In a large bowl, whisk egg yolks and sugar until thick and pale. Fold in mascarpone until smooth.
3. In a separate bowl, whip heavy cream to stiff peaks and gently fold it into the mascarpone mixture.
4. Spread half of the mascarpone mixture over the ladyfingers. Add another layer of dipped ladyfingers, then top with the remaining mascarpone mixture.
5. Refrigerate for at least 4 hours or overnight. Before serving, dust with cocoa powder and garnish with chocolate shavings.

Florentine Steak (Bistecca alla Fiorentina)

Ingredients:

- 2 large bone-in porterhouse steaks (about 2 inches thick)
- Olive oil for drizzling
- 2 sprigs fresh rosemary
- 2 cloves garlic, smashed
- Coarse sea salt and freshly ground black pepper
- 1 lemon, halved

Instructions:

1. Preheat your grill to high heat.
2. Rub the steaks with olive oil and season generously with salt and pepper. Place the rosemary sprigs and garlic cloves on the grill with the steaks.
3. Grill the steaks for 5–6 minutes per side for medium-rare, or longer for your desired doneness.
4. Remove the steaks from the grill and let them rest for 10 minutes.
5. Squeeze fresh lemon juice over the steaks before serving.

Wild Mushroom Risotto

Ingredients:

- 1 lb wild mushrooms, sliced (such as shiitake, cremini, or porcini)
- 1 ½ cups Arborio rice
- 4 cups chicken or vegetable broth
- 1 cup dry white wine
- 1 small onion, chopped
- 2 cloves garlic, minced
- 2 tbsp butter
- ¼ cup grated Parmesan cheese
- Fresh parsley, chopped
- Salt and pepper to taste

Instructions:

1. In a large skillet, melt 1 tbsp butter over medium heat. Add the mushrooms and cook until tender and browned. Set aside.
2. In a separate saucepan, heat the broth over low heat.
3. In a large pan, melt the remaining butter over medium heat. Add the onion and garlic and sauté until soft.
4. Add the rice and stir to coat. Pour in the wine and cook until absorbed.
5. Gradually add the warm broth, one ladle at a time, stirring constantly until the liquid is absorbed before adding more. Continue until the rice is tender and creamy (about 18–20 minutes).
6. Stir in the cooked mushrooms, Parmesan, and parsley. Season with salt and pepper and serve.

Pistachio Panna Cotta

Ingredients:

- 1 ½ cups heavy cream
- ½ cup whole milk
- ⅓ cup granulated sugar
- ½ tsp vanilla extract
- 2 tbsp pistachio paste or ground pistachios
- 1 packet (2 ½ tsp) unflavored gelatin
- 2 tbsp warm water

Instructions:

1. In a small bowl, sprinkle gelatin over the warm water and stir until dissolved. Set aside.
2. In a saucepan, combine cream, milk, sugar, and pistachio paste. Heat over medium heat, stirring until sugar dissolves and the mixture is warm (but not boiling).
3. Remove from heat and stir in the dissolved gelatin and vanilla extract.
4. Pour the mixture into serving glasses and refrigerate for at least 4 hours or until set.
5. Before serving, top with chopped pistachios or a drizzle of pistachio syrup.

Penne alla Vodka

Ingredients:

- 1 lb penne pasta
- 1 tbsp olive oil
- 1 small onion, finely chopped
- 2 cloves garlic, minced
- 1 can (14.5 oz) crushed tomatoes
- 1 cup heavy cream
- ¼ cup vodka
- ½ cup Parmesan cheese, grated
- Fresh basil leaves, chopped
- Salt and pepper to taste

Instructions:

1. Cook the penne according to package instructions. Drain and set aside.
2. In a large skillet, heat olive oil over medium heat. Add the onion and garlic and sauté until soft.
3. Stir in the crushed tomatoes and vodka, and simmer for 5 minutes, allowing the alcohol to cook off.
4. Lower the heat and stir in the cream. Simmer until the sauce thickens, about 5 minutes.
5. Toss the pasta with the sauce, adding Parmesan and fresh basil. Season with salt and pepper, and serve.

Zucchini Parmigiana

Ingredients:

- 4 medium zucchinis, sliced into ¼-inch rounds
- 2 cups marinara sauce
- 1 ½ cups mozzarella cheese, shredded
- ½ cup grated Parmesan cheese
- 2 tbsp fresh basil, chopped
- 1 cup breadcrumbs
- Olive oil for frying

Instructions:

1. Preheat your oven to 375°F (190°C).
2. Heat olive oil in a skillet and fry the zucchini slices until golden brown. Drain on paper towels.
3. In a baking dish, spread a thin layer of marinara sauce. Layer the zucchini, then top with sauce, mozzarella, Parmesan, and a sprinkle of basil.
4. Repeat layers until the ingredients are used up, finishing with cheese on top.
5. Bake for 25 minutes, or until bubbly and golden. Let cool slightly before serving.

Eggplant Involtini

Ingredients:

- 2 medium eggplants, sliced lengthwise into ½-inch thick strips
- 1 cup ricotta cheese
- 1 egg
- ½ cup grated Parmesan cheese
- 2 tbsp fresh basil, chopped
- 2 cups marinara sauce
- Olive oil for frying
- Salt and pepper to taste

Instructions:

1. Preheat oven to 375°F (190°C). Salt the eggplant slices and let them sit for 15 minutes to draw out moisture. Pat dry with a towel.
2. Heat olive oil in a skillet and fry the eggplant strips until golden. Drain on paper towels.
3. In a bowl, combine ricotta, egg, Parmesan, basil, salt, and pepper.
4. Spread a spoonful of the ricotta mixture on each eggplant strip and roll up tightly.
5. Place the rolls in a baking dish and cover with marinara sauce.
6. Bake for 20 minutes, or until the sauce is bubbling. Serve hot.

Fennel and Orange Salad

Ingredients:

- 1 large fennel bulb, thinly sliced
- 2 large oranges, peeled and sliced
- 1 tbsp olive oil
- 1 tbsp white wine vinegar
- Salt and pepper to taste
- Fresh parsley, chopped

Instructions:

1. In a large bowl, combine fennel and orange slices.
2. In a small bowl, whisk together olive oil, vinegar, salt, and pepper.
3. Drizzle the dressing over the fennel and orange mixture, and toss gently.
4. Garnish with fresh parsley and serve immediately.

Garlic and Herb Focaccia Bread

Ingredients:

- 3 ½ cups all-purpose flour
- 1 packet (2 ¼ tsp) active dry yeast
- 1 tsp sugar
- 1 ½ cups warm water
- ¼ cup olive oil, plus extra for drizzling
- 2 tsp sea salt, divided
- 1 tbsp fresh rosemary, chopped
- 3 cloves garlic, minced
- Coarse sea salt for topping

Instructions:

1. In a bowl, combine warm water, sugar, and yeast. Let sit for 5–10 minutes until frothy.
2. Stir in olive oil, flour, and 1 tsp salt. Knead until smooth, about 10 minutes. Cover with a towel and let rise for 1 hour or until doubled in size.
3. Preheat the oven to 400°F (200°C). Grease a baking sheet and transfer the dough onto it. Press out into a rectangular shape.
4. In a small bowl, mix garlic, rosemary, and 1 tsp salt with 2 tbsp olive oil. Drizzle this mixture over the dough, then use your fingers to create dimples in the dough.
5. Sprinkle with coarse sea salt and bake for 20–25 minutes until golden and crisp. Serve warm.

Polenta with Sausage and Mushrooms

Ingredients:

- 1 ½ cups cornmeal (polenta)
- 4 cups water or chicken broth
- 2 tbsp butter
- 1 tbsp olive oil
- 1 lb Italian sausage, casing removed
- 1 cup mushrooms, sliced (such as cremini or button)
- 1 small onion, chopped
- 2 cloves garlic, minced
- 1 cup Parmesan cheese, grated
- Salt and pepper to taste

Instructions:

1. Bring water or broth to a boil in a large pot. Gradually whisk in the cornmeal and cook, stirring constantly, until thick and creamy, about 15–20 minutes. Stir in butter and Parmesan. Set aside.
2. In a skillet, heat olive oil over medium heat. Add sausage and cook until browned, breaking it up with a spoon.
3. Add onion, garlic, and mushrooms, and cook until softened, about 5–7 minutes. Season with salt and pepper.
4. Serve the sausage and mushroom mixture over the creamy polenta. Garnish with extra Parmesan, if desired.

Shrimp Scampi Linguine

Ingredients:

- 12 oz linguine pasta
- 1 lb large shrimp, peeled and deveined
- 4 cloves garlic, minced
- ½ cup white wine
- ¼ cup lemon juice
- ¼ cup butter
- ¼ cup olive oil
- 1 tbsp fresh parsley, chopped
- Salt and pepper to taste

Instructions:

1. Cook linguine according to package instructions. Drain, reserving 1 cup of pasta water.
2. In a large skillet, heat olive oil and butter over medium heat. Add garlic and cook for 1 minute, until fragrant.
3. Add shrimp and cook for 2-3 minutes on each side until pink and opaque.
4. Pour in white wine and lemon juice, and cook for an additional 2 minutes.
5. Toss the cooked linguine with the shrimp mixture. Add reserved pasta water as needed to create a smooth sauce.
6. Season with salt, pepper, and fresh parsley before serving.

Arancini di Riso (Rice Balls)

Ingredients:

- 2 cups cooked risotto (cooled)
- 1 cup mozzarella cheese, cubed
- 2 tbsp grated Parmesan cheese
- 2 eggs, beaten
- 1 cup all-purpose flour
- 2 cups breadcrumbs
- Vegetable oil for frying
- Salt and pepper to taste

Instructions:

1. Preheat oil in a deep frying pan to 350°F (175°C).
2. In a bowl, combine the cooled risotto, mozzarella, Parmesan, and a pinch of salt and pepper. Shape the mixture into small balls, about the size of a golf ball.
3. Dredge each ball in flour, dip in beaten eggs, then coat in breadcrumbs.
4. Fry the rice balls in the hot oil for about 4–5 minutes until golden brown and crispy. Drain on paper towels.
5. Serve warm with marinara sauce for dipping.

Chicken Cacciatore

Ingredients:

- 4 bone-in, skinless chicken thighs
- 2 tbsp olive oil
- 1 onion, sliced
- 2 bell peppers, sliced
- 3 cloves garlic, minced
- 1 can (14.5 oz) crushed tomatoes
- 1 cup dry white wine
- 1 tbsp dried oregano
- 1 tbsp fresh basil, chopped
- Salt and pepper to taste

Instructions:

1. Heat olive oil in a large skillet over medium heat. Brown the chicken thighs on both sides, about 6–8 minutes. Remove and set aside.
2. In the same skillet, add onion, bell peppers, and garlic. Cook until softened, about 5 minutes.
3. Add the crushed tomatoes, white wine, oregano, basil, and a pinch of salt and pepper. Stir to combine.
4. Return the chicken to the pan, cover, and simmer for 30 minutes, or until the chicken is cooked through and tender.
5. Serve with pasta or crusty bread.

Prosciutto-Wrapped Melon

Ingredients:

- 1 cantaloupe or honeydew melon, peeled, seeded, and cut into wedges
- 8 oz prosciutto, thinly sliced
- Fresh basil leaves (optional)

Instructions:

1. Cut the prosciutto slices in half lengthwise. Wrap each melon wedge with a slice of prosciutto.
2. Arrange the wrapped melon on a platter, and garnish with fresh basil if desired.
3. Serve immediately as an appetizer.

Amaretto Biscotti

Ingredients:

- 2 cups all-purpose flour
- 1 cup sugar
- 1 tsp baking powder
- 1 tsp almond extract
- 2 large eggs
- ½ cup chopped almonds
- ¼ cup Amaretto liqueur

Instructions:

1. Preheat your oven to 350°F (175°C) and line a baking sheet with parchment paper.
2. In a bowl, mix flour, sugar, and baking powder. Add the eggs, almond extract, and Amaretto, and mix until a dough forms.
3. Stir in the chopped almonds.
4. Divide the dough into two logs on the baking sheet and flatten them slightly.
5. Bake for 25 minutes, then remove and let cool for 10 minutes. Slice the logs into ½-inch pieces and bake again for 10–12 minutes until crisp.
6. Let cool completely before serving.

Lemon Ricotta Cheesecake

Ingredients:

- 1 ½ cups graham cracker crumbs
- ¼ cup sugar
- ½ cup butter, melted
- 2 cups ricotta cheese
- 8 oz cream cheese, softened
- ¾ cup sugar
- 3 large eggs
- 2 tbsp lemon zest
- 1 tbsp lemon juice
- 1 tsp vanilla extract

Instructions:

1. Preheat the oven to 325°F (165°C). Grease a springform pan.
2. Combine graham cracker crumbs, sugar, and melted butter. Press the mixture into the bottom of the pan.
3. In a bowl, beat ricotta cheese, cream cheese, and sugar until smooth. Add eggs one at a time, beating well after each addition.
4. Stir in lemon zest, lemon juice, and vanilla extract.
5. Pour the mixture into the prepared crust and bake for 50–60 minutes, or until the center is set.
6. Let cool to room temperature, then refrigerate for at least 4 hours before serving.

Basil Pesto Genovese

Ingredients:

- 2 cups fresh basil leaves, packed
- ¼ cup pine nuts, toasted
- 2 cloves garlic, minced
- ½ cup Parmesan cheese, grated
- ¼ cup Pecorino Romano cheese, grated
- ½ cup extra virgin olive oil
- Salt and pepper to taste

Instructions:

1. In a food processor, combine basil, pine nuts, garlic, and cheeses. Pulse until finely chopped.
2. Slowly add olive oil while the processor is running, until the pesto reaches your desired consistency.
3. Season with salt and pepper to taste. Serve with pasta, bread, or as a topping for meats and vegetables.

Creamy Potato Gnocchi with Gorgonzola Sauce

Ingredients:

- 1 lb potato gnocchi (store-bought or homemade)
- 1 tbsp butter
- 1 cup heavy cream
- ½ cup Gorgonzola cheese, crumbled
- 2 tbsp Parmesan cheese, grated
- Salt and pepper to taste
- Fresh parsley for garnish

Instructions:

1. Cook the gnocchi according to package instructions. Drain and set aside.
2. In a saucepan, melt butter over medium heat. Add cream and bring to a simmer.
3. Stir in Gorgonzola cheese and cook until melted, then add Parmesan cheese. Stir until the sauce is smooth.
4. Season with salt and pepper.
5. Toss the gnocchi in the sauce until evenly coated. Garnish with fresh parsley and serve.

Calabrian Chili Oil Pasta

Ingredients:

- 12 oz spaghetti or other pasta
- 3 tbsp Calabrian chili oil
- 4 cloves garlic, minced
- 1 tsp red pepper flakes (optional)
- ½ cup grated Parmesan cheese
- Salt to taste
- Fresh basil for garnish

Instructions:

1. Cook pasta according to package instructions. Reserve 1 cup of pasta water, then drain the pasta.
2. In a large skillet, heat the Calabrian chili oil over medium heat. Add garlic and red pepper flakes, sauté for 1-2 minutes until fragrant.
3. Add the cooked pasta to the skillet and toss in the chili oil mixture. Add a bit of pasta water to help coat the pasta.
4. Stir in Parmesan cheese and season with salt. Garnish with fresh basil and serve.

Grilled Octopus Salad

Ingredients:

- 1 lb octopus, cleaned
- 1 lemon, sliced
- 2 tbsp olive oil, plus more for grilling
- 1 tbsp fresh oregano, chopped
- 2 cups arugula
- 1 cucumber, thinly sliced
- 1 red onion, thinly sliced
- Salt and pepper to taste

Instructions:

1. Preheat the grill to medium-high heat. Rub octopus with olive oil and season with salt and pepper.
2. Grill the octopus for 3–4 minutes per side, until charred and tender. Remove from the grill and slice into bite-sized pieces.
3. In a large bowl, combine arugula, cucumber, red onion, and oregano.
4. Drizzle with olive oil and lemon juice, toss to combine. Top with grilled octopus and serve immediately.

Clam and Mussel Linguine

Ingredients:

- 12 oz linguine pasta
- 1 lb clams, scrubbed
- 1 lb mussels, scrubbed
- 3 tbsp olive oil
- 4 cloves garlic, minced
- 1 cup white wine
- ½ cup chopped parsley
- Salt and pepper to taste
- Lemon wedges for serving

Instructions:

1. Cook linguine according to package instructions. Drain, reserving some pasta water.
2. In a large pot, heat olive oil over medium heat. Add garlic and cook for 1 minute.
3. Add clams, mussels, and white wine. Cover and cook for 5–7 minutes, or until the shellfish open.
4. Toss the cooked pasta in the pot with the shellfish and their juices. Add reserved pasta water if needed.
5. Stir in parsley, and season with salt and pepper. Serve with lemon wedges.

Sweet Ricotta Cannoli

Ingredients for Shells:

- 2 cups all-purpose flour
- 1 tbsp sugar
- ¼ tsp salt
- 2 tbsp unsalted butter, cold and cubed
- 1 egg
- 2 tbsp white wine
- 1 egg yolk, for egg wash
- Vegetable oil for frying

Ingredients for Filling:

- 1 ½ cups ricotta cheese, drained
- ½ cup powdered sugar
- ½ tsp vanilla extract
- 2 tbsp dark chocolate chips
- Chopped pistachios or candied fruit for garnish

Instructions:

1. For the shells, combine flour, sugar, and salt in a bowl. Add butter and rub it in until the mixture resembles breadcrumbs. Add egg and wine, mixing to form a dough.
2. Knead the dough for about 10 minutes, then wrap in plastic wrap and refrigerate for 30 minutes.
3. Roll the dough thinly and cut into 4-inch circles. Wrap each circle around a cannoli tube and brush the edges with egg yolk.
4. Heat oil in a deep pan to 350°F (175°C). Fry the shells for 2–3 minutes until golden. Remove and drain on paper towels.
5. For the filling, mix ricotta, powdered sugar, and vanilla. Stir in chocolate chips.
6. Pipe the ricotta mixture into the cooled shells and garnish with pistachios or candied fruit.

Pumpkin Ravioli with Sage Butter

Ingredients for Ravioli:

- 1 package fresh ravioli (or homemade pumpkin ravioli)
- 1 cup pumpkin puree
- 1 tbsp fresh thyme, chopped
- 1 tbsp Parmesan cheese, grated

Ingredients for Sage Butter Sauce:

- 4 tbsp unsalted butter
- 10-12 fresh sage leaves
- ¼ cup Parmesan cheese, grated
- Salt and pepper to taste

Instructions:

1. Cook the ravioli according to package instructions. Drain, reserving 1 cup of pasta water.
2. In a saucepan, melt butter over medium heat. Add sage leaves and cook until crispy, about 2 minutes.
3. Toss the cooked ravioli in the sage butter, adding pasta water to achieve a silky sauce.
4. Stir in Parmesan cheese and season with salt and pepper.
5. Serve with a sprinkle of fresh thyme and extra Parmesan cheese.

Porcini Mushroom Tagliatelle

Ingredients:

- 12 oz tagliatelle pasta
- 1 cup dried porcini mushrooms, soaked in warm water
- 1 tbsp olive oil
- 2 cloves garlic, minced
- 1 cup heavy cream
- 1 cup fresh mushrooms, sliced
- ¼ cup Parmesan cheese, grated
- Salt and pepper to taste

Instructions:

1. Cook tagliatelle according to package instructions. Drain, reserving some pasta water.
2. In a large skillet, heat olive oil over medium heat. Add garlic and cook for 1 minute until fragrant.
3. Add the soaked porcini mushrooms and fresh mushrooms, cooking for 5 minutes until soft.
4. Stir in heavy cream and Parmesan, simmer for 5–7 minutes until the sauce thickens.
5. Toss the cooked tagliatelle in the mushroom sauce, adding pasta water as needed. Season with salt and pepper.
6. Serve with additional Parmesan cheese and fresh parsley.

Classic Minestrone Soup

Ingredients:

- 2 tablespoons olive oil
- 1 medium onion, chopped
- 2 cloves garlic, minced
- 2 medium carrots, diced
- 2 celery stalks, diced
- 1 zucchini, diced
- 1 potato, peeled and diced
- 1 cup green beans, chopped into 1-inch pieces
- 1 cup canned diced tomatoes (or fresh tomatoes, chopped)
- 6 cups vegetable broth (or chicken broth for non-vegetarian)
- 1 teaspoon dried basil
- 1 teaspoon dried oregano
- Salt and pepper to taste
- 1 cup small pasta (such as elbow macaroni or ditalini)
- 1 15-ounce can of cannellini beans or kidney beans, drained and rinsed
- 1 cup fresh spinach or kale, chopped
- Freshly grated Parmesan cheese (optional, for garnish)

Instructions:

1. Heat the olive oil in a large pot over medium heat. Add the chopped onion and garlic, cooking until softened and fragrant, about 3-4 minutes.
2. Add the carrots, celery, zucchini, potato, and green beans. Stir everything together and cook for another 5-6 minutes until the vegetables start to soften.
3. Pour in the diced tomatoes and vegetable broth. Add the basil, oregano, salt, and pepper. Stir to combine, and bring the mixture to a boil. Once boiling, reduce the heat and let it simmer for about 20 minutes, or until the vegetables are tender.
4. Add the pasta and cook according to the package instructions, usually about 8-10 minutes.
5. Once the pasta is tender, stir in the beans and spinach (or kale) and cook for another 3-4 minutes until the greens are wilted.
6. Taste the soup and adjust seasoning with more salt and pepper if needed.
7. Ladle the soup into bowls and garnish with freshly grated Parmesan cheese if desired. Enjoy!

Marinated Artichokes

Ingredients:

- 6 fresh artichokes
- 2 cloves garlic, minced
- 1/4 cup red wine vinegar
- 1/2 cup olive oil
- 1 tablespoon lemon juice
- 1 teaspoon dried oregano
- Salt and pepper to taste
- Fresh parsley, chopped (for garnish)

Instructions:

1. Trim the artichokes by cutting off the top and removing the tough outer leaves. Cut them in half and remove the choke.
2. Boil the artichokes in salted water for 10-15 minutes until tender. Drain and let cool.
3. In a bowl, combine garlic, red wine vinegar, olive oil, lemon juice, oregano, salt, and pepper.
4. Place the cooled artichokes in a jar or container and pour the marinade over them. Let marinate for at least 2 hours before serving. Garnish with chopped parsley.

Italian Wedding Soup

Ingredients:

- 1 tablespoon olive oil
- 1 small onion, chopped
- 2 cloves garlic, minced
- 6 cups chicken broth
- 1 cup small pasta (like acini di pepe or orzo)
- 1 pound ground beef and pork mix
- 1/2 cup breadcrumbs
- 1/4 cup grated Parmesan cheese
- 1 egg, beaten
- 1 teaspoon dried oregano
- 2 cups fresh spinach or escarole, chopped
- Salt and pepper to taste

Instructions:

1. In a bowl, mix the ground meat, breadcrumbs, Parmesan, egg, oregano, salt, and pepper. Form small meatballs, about 1 inch in size.
2. Heat olive oil in a large pot and sauté the onion and garlic until softened, about 3-4 minutes.
3. Add the chicken broth and bring to a boil. Drop in the meatballs and simmer for about 20 minutes.
4. Add the pasta and spinach, cooking until the pasta is al dente, about 8-10 minutes. Adjust seasoning with salt and pepper.
5. Serve hot, garnished with extra Parmesan if desired.

Stuffed Bell Peppers with Italian Sausage

Ingredients:

- 4 bell peppers, tops cut off and seeds removed
- 1 pound Italian sausage, casings removed
- 1 cup cooked rice
- 1/2 cup marinara sauce
- 1/2 cup shredded mozzarella cheese
- 1/4 cup grated Parmesan cheese
- 1 tablespoon fresh basil, chopped
- Salt and pepper to taste

Instructions:

1. Preheat the oven to 375°F (190°C).
2. Brown the Italian sausage in a skillet over medium heat. Drain any excess fat.
3. In a bowl, mix the cooked rice, sausage, marinara sauce, mozzarella, Parmesan, basil, salt, and pepper.
4. Stuff the peppers with the sausage mixture and place them in a baking dish.
5. Cover with foil and bake for 30 minutes. Remove the foil and bake for an additional 10 minutes until the peppers are tender and the cheese is melted.

Ricotta-Stuffed Zucchini Blossoms

Ingredients:

- 12 zucchini blossoms
- 1/2 cup ricotta cheese
- 1/4 cup grated Parmesan cheese
- 1 egg
- 1 tablespoon fresh basil, chopped
- 1/2 teaspoon lemon zest
- Salt and pepper to taste
- Olive oil, for frying

Instructions:

1. Carefully remove the pistils from the zucchini blossoms and rinse them gently.
2. In a bowl, combine ricotta, Parmesan, egg, basil, lemon zest, salt, and pepper.
3. Stuff each blossom with the ricotta mixture, being careful not to tear the petals.
4. Heat olive oil in a pan over medium heat. Gently fry the stuffed blossoms for 2-3 minutes on each side until golden and crispy.
5. Drain on paper towels and serve immediately.

Chocolate-Hazelnut Gelato

Ingredients:

- 1 cup whole milk
- 1 cup heavy cream
- 3/4 cup sugar
- 1/2 cup cocoa powder
- 1/2 cup chocolate-hazelnut spread (like Nutella)
- 4 egg yolks
- 1 teaspoon vanilla extract

Instructions:

1. In a saucepan, heat milk, cream, sugar, and cocoa powder over medium heat, whisking until the sugar dissolves and the mixture is smooth.
2. In a bowl, whisk the egg yolks. Gradually add the warm milk mixture to the egg yolks, whisking constantly.
3. Return the mixture to the saucepan and cook over low heat, stirring constantly until it thickens enough to coat the back of a spoon (about 5 minutes).
4. Remove from heat and stir in the chocolate-hazelnut spread and vanilla extract. Let cool, then refrigerate for at least 4 hours.
5. Churn in an ice cream maker according to the manufacturer's instructions. Serve once it reaches the consistency of gelato.

Chicken Marsala

Ingredients:

- 4 boneless, skinless chicken breasts
- 1/2 cup all-purpose flour
- 4 tablespoons olive oil
- 8 ounces cremini or white mushrooms, sliced
- 3/4 cup Marsala wine
- 1/2 cup chicken broth
- 2 tablespoons butter
- Salt and pepper to taste
- Fresh parsley, chopped (for garnish)

Instructions:

1. Season the chicken breasts with salt and pepper, then dredge them in flour, shaking off the excess.
2. Heat 2 tablespoons of olive oil in a pan over medium-high heat. Cook the chicken for 5-6 minutes per side until golden brown and cooked through. Remove from the pan and set aside.
3. In the same pan, add the remaining oil and sauté the mushrooms until softened, about 5 minutes.
4. Add the Marsala wine and chicken broth, scraping up any browned bits from the pan. Simmer for 5 minutes until the sauce reduces slightly.
5. Stir in the butter and return the chicken to the pan. Simmer for an additional 5 minutes.
6. Serve the chicken with the sauce and garnish with parsley.

Amatriciana Pasta

Ingredients:

- 12 ounces pasta (spaghetti or bucatini)
- 4 ounces guanciale (or pancetta), diced
- 1/2 cup canned tomatoes, crushed
- 1/4 teaspoon red pepper flakes
- 1/4 cup Pecorino Romano cheese, grated
- Salt and pepper to taste

Instructions:

1. Cook the pasta according to package instructions, reserving 1/2 cup of pasta water.
2. In a pan, cook the guanciale over medium heat until crisp, about 5-7 minutes. Remove from the pan and set aside.
3. In the same pan, add the crushed tomatoes and red pepper flakes. Simmer for 10 minutes until the sauce thickens.
4. Toss the pasta with the sauce, adding reserved pasta water as needed to reach desired consistency.
5. Stir in the guanciale and Pecorino Romano. Serve hot, garnished with extra cheese.